SPOT

COMMUNITY HELPERS

POLICE OFFICERS

by Golriz Golkar

amicus LEARNING

lights

police dog

Look for these words and pictures as you read.

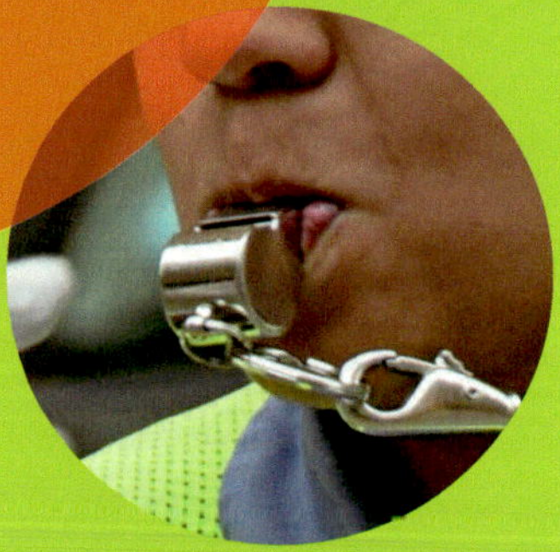

badge

whistle

Police officers help us.
What do they do?

A car drives too fast.
The lights flash.
The officer tells the
driver to pull over.

lights

57
POL

The officer has a police dog.
It works with him.
It is well trained.

badge

Uh-oh!
A man broke the law.
The officer catches him.
She shows him her badge.

POLICE

NYP

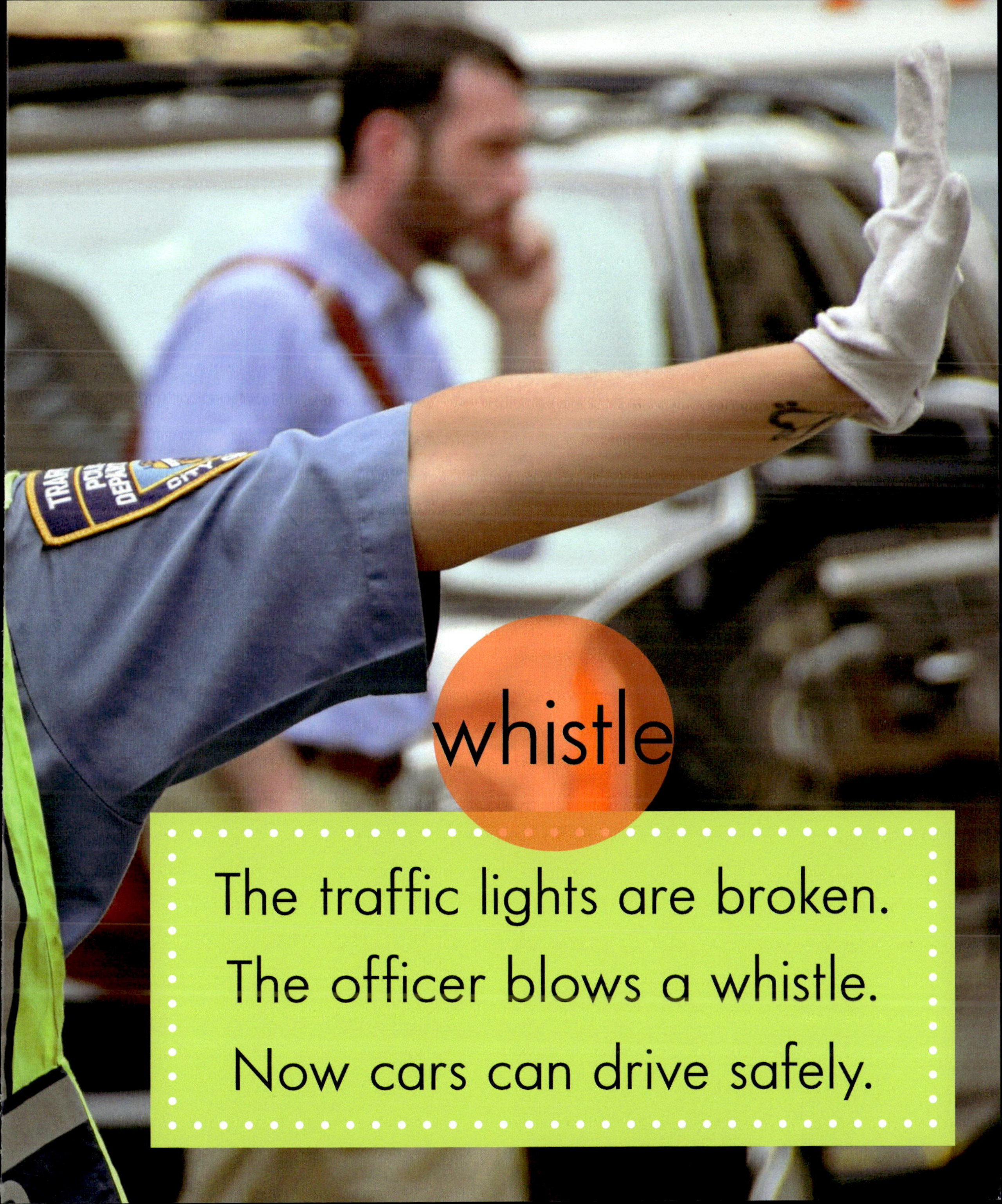

whistle

The traffic lights are broken.
The officer blows a whistle.
Now cars can drive safely.

POLICE

Ouch! Someone fell.
They are hurt.
The officer calls for help.

Police officers keep people safe. They can help us when we need it!

lights

police dog

Did you find?

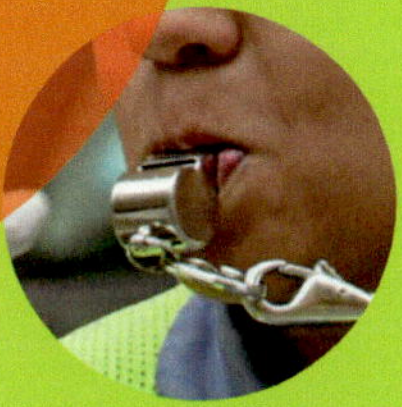

badge

whistle

Spot is published by Amicus Learning, an imprint of Amicus
P.O. Box 227, Mankato, MN 56002
www.amicuspublishing.us

Library of Congress Cataloging-in-Publication Data
Names: Golkar, Golriz, author.
Title: Police officers / by Golriz Golkar.
Description: Mankato, MN : Amicus Learning, an imprint of Amicus, [2026] | Series: Spot community helpers | Audience term: Children | Audience term: School children | Audience: Ages 4–7 | Audience: Grades K–1 | Summary: "Police officers patrol around town, control traffic, and more. Learn how they help the community in this low-level beginning reader that reinforces new vocabulary with a search-and-find feature. A great early social studies book that will inspire kindergartners and first graders to learn about jobs in their community"— Provided by publisher.
Identifiers: LCCN 2024043683 (print) | LCCN 2024043684 (ebook) | ISBN 9798892004923 (library binding) | ISBN 9798892005463 (paperback) | ISBN 9798892006002 (ebook)
Subjects: LCSH: Police—Juvenile literature. | Occupations—Juvenile literature.
Classification: LCC HV7922 .G645 2026 (print) | LCC HV7922 (ebook) | DDC 363.2–dc23/eng/20241213
LC record available at https://lccn.loc.gov/2024043683
LC ebook record available at https://lccn.loc.gov/2024043684

Ana Brauer, editor
Deb Miner, series designer
Sara Hood, book designer and photo researcher

Photos by Alamy Stock Photo/Ira Berger, 10-11; Getty Images/kali9, 3, 14; Shutterstock/antoniodiaz, 12, Gorodenkoff, 4-5, Hakim Graphy, 6-7, PeopleImages.com - Yuri A, cover, Pixel-Shot, 1, Straight 8 Photography, 8-9

POLICE OFFICERS